WHERE WE LIVE

WE LIVE IN A CITY

by Jennifer Boothroyd

Consultant: Beth Gambro
Reading Specialist, Yorkville, Illinois

Minneapolis, Minnesota

Teaching Tips

Before Reading

- Look at the cover of the book. Discuss the picture and the title.
- Ask readers to brainstorm a list of what they already know about cities. What can they expect to see in the book?
- Go on a picture walk, looking through the pictures to discuss vocabulary and make predictions about the text.

During Reading

- Read for purpose. Encourage readers to think about the city they live in as they are reading.
- Ask readers to look for the details of the book. What are they learning about the things people in a city have in common?
- If readers encounter an unknown word, ask them to look at the sounds in the word. Then, ask them to look at the rest of the page. Are there any clues to help them understand?

After Reading

- Encourage readers to pick a buddy and reread the book together.
- Ask readers to name two things they might see in a city. Find the pages that tell about these things.
- Ask readers to write or draw something they learned about living in a city.

Credits:
Cover and title page, © shutterupeire/Shutterstock; 3, © Stephen Coburn/Shutterstock; 5, © John Rowley/iStock; 6–7, © PapaBear/iStock; 8–9, © Beboy_ltd/iStock; 10–11, © marchello74/Adobe Stock; 13, © NicolasMcComber/iStock; 14, © Jeanne McRight/Shutterstock; 14–15, © THEPALMER/iStock; 17, © SDI Productions/iStock; 18–19, © Freebird7977/Shutterstock; 20–21, © Sergey Novikov/Shutterstock; 22T, © mremos/iStock; 22M, © Eloi_Omella/iStock; 22B, © Tatiana Dokolina/Shutterstock; 23TL, © Elena Elisseeva/Shutterstock; 23TR, © Monkey Business Images/Shutterstock; 23BL, © xavierarnau/iStock; 23BM, © avid_creative/iStock; 23BR, © chokkicx/iStock.

Library of Congress Cataloging-in-Publication Data is available at www.loc.gov or upon request from the publisher.

ISBN: 979-8-88822-060-3 (hardcover)
ISBN: 979-8-88822-257-7 (paperback)
ISBN: 979-8-88822-375-8 (ebook)

Copyright © 2024 Bearport Publishing Company. All rights reserved. No part of this publication may be reproduced in whole or in part, stored in any retrieval system, or transmitted in any form or by any means, electronic, mechanical, photocopying, recording, or otherwise, without written permission from the publisher.

For more information, write to Bearport Publishing, 5357 Penn Avenue South, Minneapolis, MN 55419.

Contents

Home Team 4

City Facts 22

Glossary 23

Index 24

Read More 24

Learn More Online 24

About the Author 24

Home Team

The game is about to start!

Our city has a great team.

We are ready to cheer them on.

A city is a place where people live and work.

It is in a much larger **state**.

There are many cities in each state.

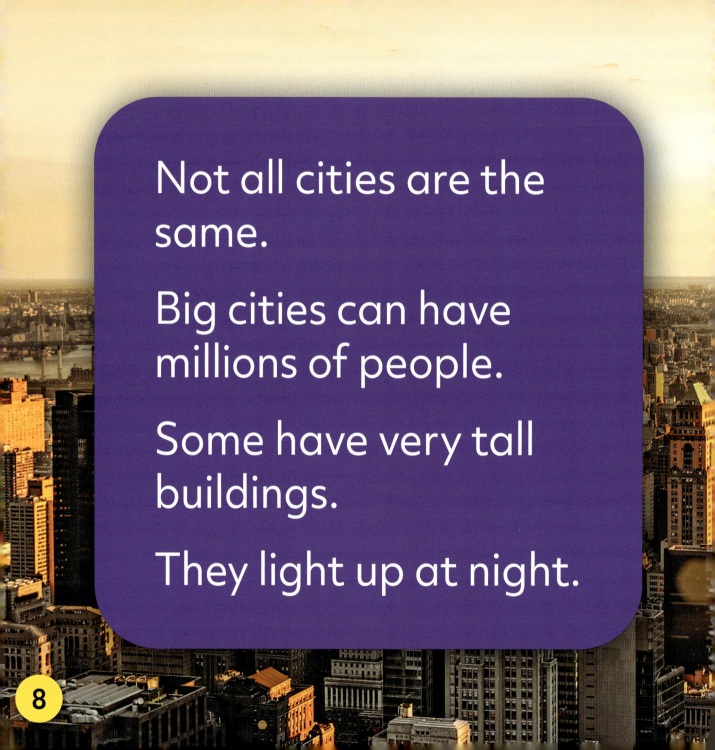

Not all cities are the same.

Big cities can have millions of people.

Some have very tall buildings.

They light up at night.

Other cities have fewer people.

They may have more space with trees and grass.

Small cities are sometimes called towns.

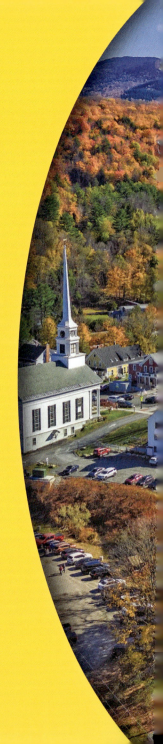

Our city is like many others.

People live in **apartments** and houses.

Shops sell things we need.

We visit the park to have fun.

We can take city buses where we need to go.

Firefighters work for our city.

They keep us safe.

The **mayor** leads our city.

She works at city hall.

Her job is to help everyone in our **community**.

We can do our part to make our city nice, too.

Help the people on your block shovel snow.

Clean up the city park.

Our city is a special place.

And we are an important part of it.

We love our city!

City Facts

Many cities have the same name. Washington and Franklin are some of the most common city names in the United States.

There are more than 37 million people in Tokyo, Japan. That's the most in the world!

Some very small towns do not really need a mayor. Sometimes, they pick animals to be mayor.

Glossary

apartments buildings with many homes inside

community a group of people that lives together or shares something in common

firefighters people whose job it is to stop fires and keep people safe

mayor a person chosen to lead a city government

state an area of land with a government that is inside a country

Index

buses 14
firefighters 14
mayor 16, 22
parks 12, 19
people 6, 8, 10, 12, 19, 22
shops 12
state 6
towns 10, 22

Read More

Gaertner, Meg. *My City (Where I Live)*. Lake Elmo, MN: Focus Readers, 2021.

Rodriguez, Alicia. *City (Where Do I Live?)*. New York: Crabtree Publishing, 2022.

Learn More Online

1. Go to **www.factsurfer.com** or scan the QR code below.
2. Enter "**In a City**" into the search box.
3. Click on the cover of this book to see a list of websites.

About the Author

Jenny Boothroyd lives in a city with 86,000 people. She grew up in a town that had 6,000 people.